FOOTBALL LEGENDS

Troy Aikman

Terry Bradshaw

Jim Brown

John Elway

Brett Favre

Michael Irvin

Vince Lombardi

John Madden

Dan Marino

Joe Montana

Joe Namath

Walter Payton

Jerry Rice

Barry Sanders

Deion Sanders

Emmitt Smith

Lawrence Taylor

Steve Young

CHELSEA HOUSE PUBLISHERS

FOOTBALL LEGENDS

MICHAEL IRVIN

Richard Rosenblatt

Introduction by
Chuck Noll

CHELSEA HOUSE PUBLISHERS
Philadelphia

Produced by Daniel Bial and Associates
New York, New York

Picture research by Alan Gottlieb
Cover illustration by Earl K. Parker III

First Printing

1 3 5 7 9 8 6 4 2

Library of Congress Cataloging-in-Publication Data

Rosenblatt, Richard.
    Michael Irvin / Richard Rosenblatt; introduction by Chuck Noll.
        p.   cm. -- (Football legends)
    Includes bibiliographical references and index.
    ISBN 0-7910-4397-5
    1. Irvin, Michael, 1966-   --Juvenile literature. 2. Football
players--United States--Biography--Juvenile literature. [1. Irvin, Michael,
1966-
    2. Football players. 3. Afro-Americans--Biography.] I. Title. II. Series.
GV939.I48R67 1997
796.332'092--dc21
[B]   96-52618
                                                                 CIP
                                                                 AC

CONTENTS

A WINNING ATTITUDE

Chuck Noll

Don't ever fall into the trap of believing, "I could never do that. And I won't even try—I don't want to embarrass myself." After all, most top athletes had no idea what they could accomplish when they were young. A secret to the success of every star quarterback and sure-handed receiver is that they tried. If they had not tried, if they had not persevered, they would never have discovered how far they could go and how much they could achieve.

You can learn about trying hard and overcoming challenges by being a sports fan. Or you can take part in organized sports at any level, in any capacity. The student messenger at my high school is now president of a university. A reserve ballplayer who got very little playing time in high school now owns a very successful business. Both of them benefited by the lesson of perseverance that sports offers. The main point is that you don't have to be a Hall of Fame athlete to reap the benefits of participating in sports.

In math class, I learned that the whole is equal to the sum of its parts. But that is not always the case when you are dealing with people. Sports has taught me that the whole is either greater than or less than the sum of its parts, depending on how well the parts work together. And how the parts work together depends on how they really understand the concept of teamwork.

Most people believe that teamwork is a fifty-fifty proposition. But true teamwork is seldom, if ever, fifty-fifty. Teamwork is *whatever it takes to get the job done.* There is no time for the measurement of contributions, no time for anything but concentrating on your job.

One year, my Pittsburgh Steelers were playing the Houston

Oilers in the Astrodome late in the season, with the division championship on the line. Our offensive line was hard hit by the flu, our starting quarterback was out with an injury, and we were having difficulty making a first down. There was tremendous pressure on our defense to perform well—and they rose to the occasion. If the players on the defensive unit had been measuring their contribution against the offense's contribution, they would have given up and gone home. Instead, with a "whatever it takes" attitude, they increased their level of concentration and performance, forced turnovers, and got the ball into field goal range for our offense. Thanks to our defense's winning attitude, we came away with a victory.

Believing in doing whatever it takes to get the job done is what separates a successful person from someone who is not as successful. Nobody can give you this winning outlook; you have to develop it. And I know from experience that it can be learned and developed on the playing field.

My favorite people on the football field have always been offensive linemen and defensive backs. I say this because it takes special people to perform well in jobs in which there is little public recognition when they are doing things right but are thrust into the spotlight as soon as they make a mistake. That is exactly what happens to a lineman whose man sacks the quarterback or a defensive back who lets his receiver catch a touchdown pass. They know the importance of being part of a group that believes in teamwork and does not point fingers at one another.

Sports can be a learning situation as much as it can be fun. And that's why I say, "Get involved. Participate."

CHUCK NOLL, the Pittsburgh Steelers head coach from 1969–1991, led his team to four Super Bowl victories — the most by any coach. Widely respected as an innovator on both offense and defense, Noll was inducted into the Pro Football Hall of Fame in 1993.

1

IRVIN'S GREATEST GAME

The first championship is usually the sweetest. In Michael Irvin's case, his first National Football League (NFL) championship was indeed the best, which is why the Dallas Cowboys' sensational wide receiver ranks Super Bowl XXVII as his most memorable and greatest game.

Irvin had already won a college national championship at the University of Miami. In just three years there, he set Miami career records for catches, yards, and touchdown passes. In his four years as a professional, he had already become one of the most well-known and well-respected players in the NFL. But winning that first Super Bowl proved to be a springboard to even more success for the acrobatic receiver who is rated among the best in NFL history.

"That was a game I looked forward to ever since I left Miami." Irvin said. "I knew when I went to

Michael Irvin (front) is elated after catching a touchdown pass in the 1993 Super Bowl. Fellow wide receiver Alvin Harper races over to join the celebration. Eighteen seconds later, Irvin would have another reason to be happy.

9

the Cowboys we would win a championship. It was just a matter of time. That game was special. It was the first one."

It was a perfect day for a Super Bowl. Gorgeous and sunny, with a crowd of 98,374 packed into the Rose Bowl in Pasadena, California. And the Dallas Cowboys were a team who believed they could not be beaten. Irvin, one of the most confident and charismatic players in the game, gave an indication of what was to come, when he made these remarks before the game.

"See this championship," he said, displaying the ring he won at Miami. "I had to replace the phony diamonds with real diamonds. The coaches at Miami got the ones with real diamonds in it. This ring will be replaced by another one on Sunday."

Fans around the country were looking forward to an exciting game. The Buffalo Bills were clearly the class of the American Football Conference (AFC) and this was their third trip to the Super Bowl in a row. The New York Giants had won a squeaker, 20-19, two years before, and the Washington Redskins had piled on with a 37-24 victory in 1992. Now Buffalo wanted a ring of its own, and with Bruce Smith and Cornelius Bennett leading a strong defense and a quick-scoring offense led by quarterback Jim Kelly, running back Thurman Thomas, and wide receiver Andre Reed, many football analysts thought they had a good shot at winning the game.

But the Cowboys were well-staffed at all the key positions too. Troy Aikman had established himself as the best young quarterback in the NFL and Emmitt Smith had led the league in rushing three years straight. Of course, the Cow-

Quarterback Troy Aikman's running and pin-point accuracy throwing earned him the MVP Award during the 1993 Super Bowl.

boys were also blessed by the skills of Michael Irvin, and his fellow wide receiver, Alvin Harper, had also shown game-breaking skills.

The Bills started out strong and the Cowboys seemed to have the jitters. Buffalo marched down field on their opening possession and Thurman Thomas scored on a 2-yard run to give the Bills a 7-0 lead. Dallas found its composure and tied the score on quarterback Troy Aikman's 23-yard scoring pass to tight end Jay Novacek. Then the Bills got the jitters, fumbling on their own 2 yard-line. Jimmie Jones's touchdown gave the Cowboys their first lead, but the Bills pulled within 14-10 late in the second quarter on Steve Christie's 21-yard field goal.

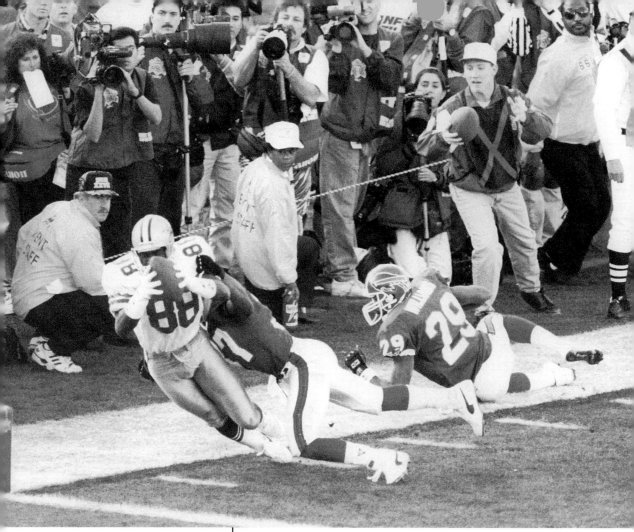

Michael Irvin has already beaten the Buffalo Bills' double coverage. Now Nate Odomes is desperately trying to get Irvin out of bounds. But Irvin makes sure both his feet have touched the ground and readies himself for a stretch that will bring the ball over the end line. This mighty feat turned into Irvin's second touchdown pass of the day.

Up until this point, Aikman was inconsistent at best as the Bills' defense shook up the Cowboys by playing a two-deep zone. On every likely passing down, they kept two defensive backs lined up deep to prevent Irvin and Alvin Harper from breaking a big play. But Irvin was about to prove he can be kept quiet for only so long.

As the Cowboys recognized Buffalo's plans, they adapted their offense. With Irvin keeping the defensive backs out of the play with his fakes, Emmitt Smith found room to make a big gainer. He slashed 38 yards to the Bills' 19 yardline. Irvin then threw a hard inside move at cornerback Nate Odomes, who spun around just in time to see Irvin snare Aikman's pass that gave the Cowboys' a 21-10 lead. The scoring sequence was quick, like a lightning bolt.

"It was a simple slant route," Irvin recalled. "I knew I had one-on-one coverage and Troy did his job and spotted it. Odomes had no help in the middle of the field. I saw six points. I knew once I got up in his face and he was leaning outside, all I had to do was catch the ball."

After the ensuing kickoff, Thurman Thomas fumbled on the first play and the Cowboys recovered on the Bills' 18 yardline. On the next play, Dallas offensive coordinator Norv Turner called for a post-corner route to Irvin.

"Mike was supposed to take three steps on a post route [before breaking toward the middle of the endzone], but he got excited and took just one big step," Turner said. " So Troy had to throw much quicker than he was supposed to."

Aikman spotted Irvin at the 3 yardline. The pass was on its way and cornerback James Williams tried to cut it off.

"I was saying 'OK ball, get here,' " Irvin said. "When he missed, that's when I knew I could get in."

Irvin caught the ball and dived into the endzone. Touchdown, Cowboys! Dallas 28, Buffalo 10. The game had swung in dramatic fashion on Irvin's touchdown catches.

"Two touchdowns in 18 seconds," marveled Irvin. "Man, that's sweet."

Irvin's heroics had sunk the Bills. Buffalo could do little right in the second half and the Cowboys added three touchdowns in a span of 2:33 of the fourth quarter and rolled to a 52-17 victory.

Irvin finished the game with six catches for 114 yards and the two touchdowns. Usually when a receiver has over 100 yards and a touchdown or two, he'll be satisfied he made a real contribution to his team's offense. But statistics can never fully tell how good a game a receiver has had. For Irvin, this Super Bowl was a defining moment in his blossoming career. Not only did he play well, but he made big catches in the big game and it led to bigger and better things for him, both on and off the field.

It also gave Irvin, along with his coach, Jimmy Johnson, his first NFL championship after a college football national title in 1987.

"This is it, better than the national championship," Irvin said in the victorious Cowboys' lockerroom. "I was thinking about it on the field, about how with coach Johnson we won the national championship and the Super Bowl.

"There's me and 46 more players in here and 12 or 13 coaches who have dreamed the same dream. And here it came true, in this fashion. I can't sit here and put it in words. You dream about the moment—actually, it's a fantasy. You get in the playoffs, it's a dream. You get here and win it, it's a reality. I just can't put it in words."

So when the game ended, it was left for Irvin to show his excitement when he approached Johnson. After Johnson's celebrated hairdo received a victorious ice water dousing, Irvin ran up to Johnson and ruffled the coach's hair with his hands. Not even control freak Johnson was upset.

"He got me pretty good," a smiling Johnson said. "I wasn't anticipating this one and he messed my hair up good."

Right then, Irvin knew the future was bright for him in Dallas.

"We're a very tight team," he said. "Everybody gets along because everybody wants the same thing. That's one of the great things about our team. We all discuss and listen to each other. Then, we can say, 'Hey, coach,' and they listen. Jimmy makes sure everybody is working in the same direction."

He also thought about winning under Johnson in college and in the pros.

"When I'm 50 and he's 89 or 90 or whatever," Irvin said, laughing, "we'll be able to look back and joke about it. We can say, 'We did it on both levels. Man, ain't that something?'"

After the game, Irvin exults with his coach, Jimmy Johnson. Johnson had just been doused with water, but that didn't seem to ruffle his hair at all.

2
GROWING UP

Michael Jerome Irvin was born on March 5, 1966, in Fort Lauderdale, Florida, 10 months before the first Super Bowl was played and six years before the Dallas Cowboys won their first NFL championship.

When Michael was born, he had plenty of company. There were 14 brothers and sisters waiting for him, and the two children born to Pearl and Walter Irvin after Michael made for a cozy family of 17 children. Michael had four brothers, two half-brothers, and 10 sisters to watch his every step growing up.

Cozy is the right word, as the Irvins lived in a moderate-sized home in a middle class black neighborhood in Fort Lauderdale.

"We were quite a family," Irvin recalled. "We were about the biggest one around. We didn't have a lot, but my Mom and Dad always worked hard to get us what we needed. Somehow, things had a way of working out."

Michael Irvin grew up in Fort Lauderdale, one of Florida's most famous beach cities.

As a kid, Michael's greatest inspiration was his father. Walter Irvin was a Baptist minister, with parishes in Fort Lauderdale, Fort Myers, Florida, and Andersonville, Georgia. That gave the Irvins a firm religious background. To feed and clothe his family, Walter spent the rest of his time as a roofer, often working 12 hours a day. All the boys were roofers, too. Michael learned the trade by going up on the roof with his father and older brothers. Roofing is hard labor, especially in the hot summer months down south.

In junior high, Michael recalled, he decided he wasn't interested in going to school, and his father told him if he wasn't going to class, he'd have to work. "So I went out on the roof a couple of days," Michael said. "After that I said, 'Dad, I want to go to school. I want to be a scholar.'"

Walter's work ethic is what Michael remembers most. And he says it greatly influenced him as he was growing up. Still does. No matter how flashy Irvin may seem on or off the field, be it touchdown celebrations on the field or showing off his dazzling jewelry off the field, he always speaks from the heart about his father.

He sometimes tells the story about when his father held a lit firecracker as it exploded in his hand. "He laughed," Irvin recalled. "We thought he was indestructible, that nothing could ever hurt him."

But when Michael was 17, and on the verge of becoming a high school star in football and basketball, his father died of cancer. Walter died on September 13, 1983 when he was only 54. He died just three days before Michael's first football game as a senior at St. Thomas Aquinas High School.

Irvin remembered his father's final days. "Toward the end, I'd take my father to the doctor for visits," Irvin once told *The Miami Herald*. "One time I heard him say, 'I don't know if I can take this anymore.' That was the biggest blow to me, hearing him say that. It's like he was quitting. I didn't understand it at the time."

All of Irvin's records at the University of Miami are dedicated to his father, the man he lovingly refers to as "Rev." And Irvin now directs his energies toward providing for his entire family. He knows what they all went through.

"Growing up, you got one pair of shoes that had to last a year or more," he said. "Your feet outgrew 'em so you'd cut the top of the shoes open. I never will forget that."

Nor will he forget one of the last conversations he had with his father. "He said, 'Michael, you've got to grow up. It's time to start being a man,' " Irvin recalled during an interview last season. "He said, 'Mike, I feel like I'm going home on the morning train, and I want you to promise to take care of your mother.' And I'm thinking, 'Sheesh, 36 brothers and sisters, what are you putting this on me for?'

"I thought everything would be fine, but he died the next morning. But I did make that promise, and I am holding up to it."

Nothing really came easy for Irvin, even in athletics. After his sophomore year, it was clear Irvin had the potential to excel in football and basketball. But his high school situation became very difficult. He could have attended Dillard

In high school, Irvin was a standout at both football and basketball.

High, a predominantly black high school near his home, but he was bused miles away to Piper High School. There were more problems.

"I was real hyper then," Irvin recalled. "There was some racism. I didn't want to acknowledge a lot of those things. Maybe I hung out with the wrong crowd. I had a quick temper then. The first thing I used to do was hit somebody. I got in a lot of fights."

According to *The Miami Herald*, when Irvin was a sophomore, he hit a female student and was suspended. With the help of his father, he transferred to St. Thomas Aquinas, a parochial school. But Piper claimed he was recruited and would not sign the transfer papers. Irvin had to sit out his junior year, unable to participate in sports, but his father considered it a victory.

Three days before Irvin began his senior season at St. Thomas, Walter Irvin passed away. Almost immediately, Irvin changed. The anger subsided. No more bad attitude. Now there was a purpose.

He had an exemplary season as he starred for his new high school team. He caught 59 passes for 987 yards and 12 touchdowns and was selected to the All-State team. His play was so impressive, he was offered scholarships by Syracuse, Miami, Louisiana State, and Michigan State.

He was really tempted to go to Syracuse University, but family ties to south Florida were too strong. The University of Miami was the choice and Irvin, who always wanted to be a star, was on his way to college.

"I'm real excited, but I've got to admit I'm more nervous than anything," he said on the day he signed his national letter of intent to attend Miami. "Playing for Miami is the big thing in the area. I remember when I was younger and Miami didn't have such good records. I said to myself that when I got there, we'd be a winner and win a national championship. They won it a year early, but I think we can win another one."

The timing, for a change, was perfect. Michael Irvin was about to step into a college football program that had just won its first national championship in 1983 and was about to embark on a run of success that would make the Hurricanes one of the most talented teams in the game.

3
MIAMI MANIA

Once again, the University of Miami was able to keep one of the state's best players from leaving home. Irvin, the teenager with the 24-hour-a-day smile, was probably the happiest recruit Miami ever had. Even though he was a high school star, Irvin was mature enough to realize he had to wait for his chance.

When he enrolled at Miami, he was well aware that he was one of four new wide receivers to go along with five upperclassmen, including All-American Eddie Brown and Stanley Shakespeare. It didn't take much to figure out that Irvin would be redshirted his freshman season. (Redshirting means that for one year an athlete can practice with the team but not play in a game. It allows a player to learn and develop without losing a year of eligibility.)

David Vickers (left) finds a good way to prevent Michael Irvin from scoring is to grab him with both hands. The strategy did not work well as Irvin's University of Miami team defeated Vickers's University of Oklahoma 20-14 in the 1988 Orange Bowl.

Sitting may have been the best thing that ever happened to Irvin. The Hurricanes football program was undergoing a dramatic change. After coach Howard Schnellenberger had led the team to its first national championship, capped off with a thrilling 31-30 win over the University of Nebraska in the Orange Bowl, he resigned to taking a coaching job in the United States Football League.

That surprising move left Miami athletic director Sam Jankovich, who had recently taken over that job, in the lurch. He went out and hired Oklahoma State coach Jimmy Johnson, and part of the deal called for Johnson to keep on any of Schnellenberger's assistants who chose to remain. Most did and as the 1984 season evolved, it became clear there were many disagreements between Johnson and his inherited assistants.

The 1984 season included some of the most exciting college games ever played, but Miami was on the losing end every time. In a game against Boston College, quarterback Doug Flutie threw a long bomb on the last play of the game, hoping a teammate—anyone—might catch it. Amazingly, his prayer was answered, and the touchdown gave Boston College a big upset. Flutie's "Hail Mary" throw became known as one of the great sports miracles of the decade. But as if that weren't enough, Miami lost to the University of Maryland 42-40 after leading 31-0 at halftime. It was the greatest comeback in college football history.

Miami finished the season with an 8-5 record after one more heartbreaking loss—a 39-37 defeat by UCLA in the Fiesta Bowl.

While Irvin took in all the controversy, he was busy getting himself ready to become a starter.

In spring practice, with most the coaching problems solved as Johnson brought in his own assistants and kept the ones he was comfortable working with, including offensive coordinator Gary Stevens and receivers coach Hubbard Alexander, Irvin worked as hard as anyone to impress his teachers.

"Late in the '84 season, coach Stevens asked me if I wanted to be redshirted," Irvin recalled. "But he also told me I had the talent to play at this level right now and that he'd try to get me in some games if I wanted to pass up the redshirt year. I knew I wouldn't play that much, I mean Eddie and Stanley are great receivers, so I decided to wait until next year."

By fall practice, with Brown and Shakespeare departed, Irvin was penciled in as a starter, with Brian Blades, who played with Irvin at Piper High School, set as the other wide receiver.

"I'm trying to be cool, laid back and relaxed and all that stuff, but the time is almost here," Irvin said. "My chance is here and man I can taste it. I can't wait."

Irvin was not the only one who wanted to make a good impression in his first game. The Hurricanes had a new quarterback, Vinnie Testaverde. He replaced the very popular Bernie Kosar who was now playing for the Cleveland Browns. Testaverde and Irvin would have an excellent opportunity to show their skills in their first game, as their opponents were the University of Florida Gators, Miami's biggest rival.

"I've got one brother who went to Florida and he and the rest of my family have been bugging me all the time," he said. "If they don't call me every day, they're calling me every other day. They keep telling me this is my big chance and

Irvin first got to know Coach Jimmy Johnson at the University of Miami. Vinny Testaverde (right) was the Hurricanes' star quarterback.

that they remembered how I did so well in big games in high school. Everyone is excited for me and I've got to say I'm pretty excited, too."

On September 7, 1985, Irvin played in his first college game. Miami had few heroes in the game as Florida won, 35-23, before a crowd of 80,227 at the Orange Bowl. For the record, Irvin caught one pass for 9 yards and left with a sprained toe. In all, the wide receivers only caught 9 of 24 pass completions because the Florida defense keyed on Miami's trio of wideouts—Irvin, Blades, and Brett Perriman.

The following week, against Rice University, Irvin gave a preview of what was to come. He caught his first touchdown pass—a 39-yarder in the second period—and finished with four catches for 73 yards. In his third game, a 45-10 win over Boston College, Irvin had his first 100-yard plus game—seven catches for 116 yards and a 16-yard scoring catch. After another win, over Cincinnati, and another scoring catch, Irvin and Miami faced another big game. The University of Oklahoma was ranked number three in the nation, and Miami would have to try to beat them on the road—in Norman, Oklahoma.

When Jimmy Johnson coached at Oklahoma State, he was never able to beat Barry Switzer's Sooners, losing all five times they met. But now he had a team capable of beating them, and Irvin would be a big part of the game plan.

Irvin got the Hurricanes going on their second possession of the game. He beat cornerback Derrick White along the sideline and caught a 56-yard touchdown pass from Testaverde just six minutes into the game. The catch was the first of many records Irvin would set. This reception gave him a school record of five straight games in which he caught a touchdown pass. In his first six games, Irvin already was Miami's leading receiver with 24 catches for 422 yards and five touchdowns. Miami upset the Sooners 27-14.

The next big game was against Florida State. Irvin again was up to the task as he made every clutch catch necessary to lead Miami's 35-27 comeback victory over the Seminoles. With the Hurricanes trailing 27-21 early in the fourth quarter, Testaverde hit Irvin with a 22-yard completion on 3rd-and-15. On the next play, Irvin got free for a 30-yard touchdown catch and the

Hurricanes went ahead, 28-27 with 9:55 left in the game.

He helped seal Miami's seventh straight win with a 32-yard catch on a third-and-20 from the Miami 13 yardline. The Hurricanes won their next two games, beating Maryland and handing Notre Dame its worst defeat since 1944 with a 58-7 drubbing.

Miami finished the regular season at 10-1, with a number two ranking. Irvin was one of the major factors. He finished with scoring catches in eight straight games (tying an NCAA record), had 46 catches for a team-best 840 yards, and a school-tying record of nine touchdowns. He also gained a reputation as one of the most expressive players on the field, unafraid to show his emotions after a big catch or a near-miss. Highlight films usually had a clip of Irvin running through the endzone after scoring and near the stands so he could celebrate with the fans.

Miami's excellent season earned them a berth in the Sugar Bowl to play the University of Tennessee. During his week in New Orleans, Irvin reflected on what had happened to him since his father passed away.

"When I point my arms to the sky after I score a touchdown, the first thing I think about is that I wish my father could be here in the flesh watching," he said. "I want to be the best wide receiver I can be and that's why I've dedicated this season, and my career, to my father."

Miami had only a slim chance of winning the national championship. But that chance never materialized as the Hurricanes were soundly beaten 35-7 by Tennessee. Meanwhile, Oklahoma beat Penn State 25-10 in the Orange Bowl and the Sooners were national champs.

Irvin summed up the game this way: "It wasn't the crowd noise, it wasn't anything. Sometimes you try and try and try and nothing goes right."

In 1986, everything went right for Irvin and the Hurricanes until the Fiesta Bowl, where Miami and Penn State, both undefeated, met for the national championship. The Nittany Lions escaped with a 14-10 win and won the title. Off the field, though, Miami's image suffered as several players got into trouble before the season and then caused an uproar when many of them showed up at the Fiesta Bowl wearing combat fatigues. Irvin was not thrilled that his team was now being perceived as the bad guys.

Speed and good hands aren't the only traits a good receiver needs. Irvin has always stressed his weight-training practices.

In fact, with the preseason scrutiny and sour headlines that followed the team around, Irvin was grateful for the season to begin. He even came up with a battle cry before Miami's opening game against South Carolina. "You know, none of that matters to us," he said of all the negative publicity surrounding the team. "We have this feeling that it's us against the world. And that we're going to win."

He said several dozen players attended church together to get ready for the season. "That's not something we always do," he said. "But we just felt we needed to get closer, get a unity thing going after all we've been through."

It worked, too. The Hurricanes went 11-0—the first perfect season in their 60-year history—and Irvin again was a center of attention. In Miami's final game, a 36-10 win over East Carolina, Geoff Torretta subbed for the injured Testaverde and threw two touchdown passes to Irvin. For the day, Irvin had eight catches for 194 yards—the second biggest single-game receiving yardage total in school history. While Testaverde went on to win the Heisman Trophy in 1986, Irvin finished the season with 53 catches for 868 yards and a school record of 11 touchdowns as Miami marched to its title showdown against Penn State.

After two seasons—the same number Brown played—Irvin had surpassed Brown's marks for career receiving yards and touchdowns.

But the season ended the same way it did the previous year, with Miami losing, this time in the Fiesta Bowl. Penn State won the game and the national title, while the Hurricanes were disappointed again. The loss was a bitter one, but there was Irvin, explaining why it wasn't the end of the world.

"Nobody's perfect," he said after Testaverde threw five interceptions and receivers dropped more passes than usual. "You're going to drop passes. No, they didn't do anything on defense we hadn't seen. They played a zone and dropped four linebackers deep, and it worked well."

A few minutes later, there was Irvin in the locker room with team chaplain, Father Leo Armbrust. They were holding hands.

"People say football is just a game and somebody has got to win and somebody has got to lose. To us, it was like a life-and-death situation. The running was going good, maybe we should have stuck with it more. But then people would say 'why didn't you pass it more?' I don't know what more we could have done differently."

In the two years Irvin had started for Miami, the Hurricanes were 21-1 in the regular season. But they were 0-2 in bowl games and had no national titles. Still, Irvin did not shy away from predicting the Hurricanes were about to win a national title.

While Irvin and the Hurricanes were able to overcome adversity off the field as the 1987 season started, problems arose about the team's on-field behavior, with several schools accusing the Miami players of taunting and insulting their players. Irvin, one of the most demonstrative players in the game, was amused by all the accusations.

"Just about every defense in the country does it—I know all the good ones do," Irvin said, referring to the intimidation factor. "It's an everyday part of the game. Florida State did it, with Deion Sanders and those guys. 'C'mon boy, you can't block better than that?' Everybody talks. Jarvis Williams of Florida, he was another one. And don't you think Oklahoma runs their mouth? It's part of football."

In the final regular season game, at home in the Orange Bowl against South Carolina, Irvin turned a short pass from Steve Walsh into a 46-yard touchdown play that put Miami ahead 7-6 in a game they would hang on to win 20-16. Irvin brandished the ball in front of the defender the final 15-20 yards. It seemed senseless, but the irrepressible Irvin was letting his excitement get the better of him.

Irvin had a lot to be excited about. For the third straight year, Miami made a great run at the national championship. Although Vinnie Testaverde left to become a member of the Tampa Bay Buccaneers, he was replaced by an adept Steve Walsh. The Hurricanes again went through the season undefeated to become the decade's only college football team besides Penn State to deliver back-to-back perfect regular seasons.

Irvin's statistics in 1987 did not surpass his numbers of the previous year, but Michael was happy to be in position to win that elusive national title. He led the team in all receiving categories with 44 catches for 715 yards and six touchdowns. His best games were against Miami's toughest opponents—132 yards against Florida State and 121 against South Carolina. His ability to make something happen when the team needed it the most explains why the press gave him the nickname, "The Playmaker."

All college football fans tuned in to the Orange Bowl to see the second-ranked Hurricanes battle for the national championship against number-one-ranked Oklahoma. And this time, the Hurricanes finally broke through and won it all. The Hurricanes beat Oklahoma 20-14.

After the game, Irvin had a difficult decision. Even though he had one more year of eligibility, he was considering leaving Miami for the National Football League.

"I don't think he'll be back," Miami's offensive coordinator Gary Stevens said. "He'll graduate, and then what's he got to come back for?"

In three seasons at Miami, Irvin had set career records for catches (143), receiving yards (2,423), and touchdown receptions (26). His 11 touchdown catches in 1986 also set a school record.

"I hear it all the time: 'Man, how much money those pros offering you?' " Irvin said. "They think people come up to me with a suitcase filled with $2 million if I'll leave college right now. People don't understand."

Pro scouts understood. Irvin was a top prospect. He was fast—not exceptionally fast, but his long, loping strides and ability to spring off his feet to make a catch made him a hot commodity. Irvin ran the 40-yard dash in 4.55 seconds, which is well below the times of many speed merchants teams like to put out at the wide receiver position. But Irvin knew how to position himself and use his body to shield defenders as well as anyone in the game. He fought for every ball and once he caught the ball he was an elusive runner. At 6'2", 205 pounds, he clearly had the size as well as the hands, speed, and routes to be a first-round draft pick.

"I think he's a low first-rounder if he comes out after this season and maybe one of the top six or seven picks in the draft if he plays a fifth year," Dallas Cowboys' talent scout Gil Brandt said. "Either way, he will play in the National Football League."

A big factor in Irvin's decision involved winning a college championship. Before the Orange Bowl win against Oklahoma, Irvin, who loves jewelry, said, "I've seen rings I'd love to buy, but... I'm waiting for a national championship ring."

Now that he had that ring, Irvin was set for the next step: the NFL.

4

I'M A COWBOY

As draft day approached, it became apparent Irvin was among the premiere receivers in the country. Michael was upbeat from the start, confident that whoever selected him would have themselves the best receiver in the world. That was typical of Irvin—but he backed up his boasts by being confident, charismatic, and a clutch performer.

The Cowboys used their 11th pick in the first round to select Irvin. Two wide receivers had already been chosen—Sterling Sharpe by the Green Bay Packers and Tim Brown by the Raiders. After he was selected, Irvin, smiling from ear-to-ear, looked right into a TV camera and said: "Go tell Danny White [the Cowboys quarterback] I'm going to put him in the Pro Bowl."

Ordinarily, it's the coaches who get doused with champagne after a big win. But friends and family let the bubbly flow freely after hearing that Michael had been picked in the first round of the NFL draft by the Dallas Cowboys.

The Cowboys changed their losing ways when they drafted Michael Irvin in 1988, Troy Aikman (left) in 1989, and Emmitt Smith (right) in 1990.

Once again, brash words from Irvin, but words he knew he could back up given the opportunity. As Cowboys president Tex Schramm said at the time: "This will speed our return to the living." He meant that it was time to turn on the publicity machine; Irvin was coming to Irving, to play in Texas Stadium.

Unlike Irvin's teams at Miami, the Cowboys were on the downswing, having finished the previous two seasons under .500. The 1988 season was even worse as Dallas finished 3-13—its worst record since the Cowboys entered the league in

1960. Tom Landry had been the only Dallas's coach in history, but he no longer had the on-field talent that helped him make it to the Super Bowl five times.

In the 1970s, the Cowboys were a dominating team, making it to the Super Bowl five times. Don Meredith, Craig Morton, and especially Roger Staubach were great quarterbacks, but they also had top-flight wide receivers to throw to.

Lance Rentzel, Drew Pearson, Lance Alworth, and "Bullet" Bob Hayes were some of the out-standing pass-catchers on those Dallas teams. Hayes was "the world's fastest man," having won the 100 meter dash at the Olympics before turn-ing pro. Billy Joe DuPree, Mike Ditka, and Jean Fuget starred at tight end.

Many of these players continued to dazzle the crowds into the early and mid 1980s. But by the time Michael Irvin came on the scene, it had been several years since Dallas had had a poten-tial Hall of Famer at wide receiver.

Irvin became the first Cowboys rookie receiv-er to start a season-opener since "Bullet" Bob Hayes did in 1965. To punctuate that start, Irvin caught a 35-yard touchdown pass from backup quarterback Steve Pelluer against the Pittsburgh Steelers. Dallas lost the game, 24-21, but Irvin was a shining star for the once-proud Cowboys.

After missing two games with a sprained ankle, he came back and caught six passes for 149 yards and two touchdowns in a late-season 24-17 victory over the Washington Redskins. What made his effort more impressive was that he was covered by Redskins All-Pro cornerback Darrell Green. It marked his first 100-yard game and his first multi-touchdown game as a pro.

Irvin finished his rookie season with 32 catches for 654 yards and five touchdowns for a team that won just three games. He led the NFC in average yards per catch at 20.4.

If Irvin thought the transition from college to pro ball was difficult, he was in for a big shock. Before the 1989 season began, there were big changes in Dallas. Owner Bum Bright sold the team to Jerry Jones, an oilman from Arkansas, and the new owner promptly fired Landry and his staff and replaced him with his good friend and old teammate Jimmy Johnson—Irvin's college coach.

With Jones and Johnson running the show, the Cowboys planned to turn around the team's fortunes as quickly as possible. While Johnson once confided to former Cowboys player personnel director Gil Brandt that he thought Irvin was a bit slow and a second-round draft pick at best, the new coach had grown to respect Irvin's work ethic.

"Nobody on this team works harder," Johnson said.

Johnson began wheeling and dealing for players. In 1989, the Cowboys made UCLA quarterback Troy Aikman their number one draft pick. Also in that draft, Dallas chose running back Daryl Johnson, defensive end Tony Tolbert, and offensive lineman Mark Stepnoski, three more talented players who would play major roles in the team's turnaround. The Cowboys also picked Miami quarterback Steve Walsh later in the supplemental draft.

Johnson's first season was not pretty, but he was not dismayed as Aikman and his other fresh faces gained experience under fire. Irvin, just starting to learn the tendencies of Aikman, was

Irvin throws a tantrum after a referee ruled he had not caught the ball. Irvin's temper sometimes got him in trouble on the field.

off to a terrific second season with 26 catches for 378 yards and two touchdowns in six games before he suffered the first big injury of his career. In the sixth game, against San Francisco, he tore his anterior cruciate ligament in his right knee and missed 14 games—the final 10 of the 1989 season and the first four of the 1990 season.

Irvin missed little interesting action while injured. The 1989 Cowboys won only one game all season long. Aikman had a tough time adjusting to the pro game, getting sacked often and suffering concussions and a broken finger.

Irvin was determined to make a complete recovery, so he went about his rehabilitation with the determination he showed on the field. He worked and worked and worked, undergoing treatment and using weights to strengthen the knee.

The end of the season was a relief. The Cowboys looked forward to the draft and to improving their fortunes. Even though the Cowboys lost their first-round pick by taking Walsh in the supplemental draft, they still had a number one pick thanks to an earlier blockbuster trade that sent Herschel Walker to the Minnesota Vikings. The Vikings, who sent over many talented players as well as draft picks in order to get the seriously muscled Walker, hoping he would be the final piece in their run for the Super Bowl, got the far worse end of the deal. When Dallas used one of the draft picks to select Florida running back Emmitt Smith, it became obvious that Minnesota had paid much too much for much too little.

The Cowboys staff had to be commended for picking Irvin in 1988, Aikman in 1989, and Smith in 1990. But all was not going well for Irvin, though. In training camp, he appeared to have lost a step during his rehab, and the Cowboys placed him on injured reserve to start the season, meaning he would miss the first four games.

In fact, the Cowboys actually contemplated trading him. Reports at the time indicated that offensive coordinator David Shula wanted to unload Irvin, while John Wooten, personnel director at the time, said he was asked to shop Irvin around. Jimmy Johnson, however, had the last word. He knew Irvin at Miami and knew he could be a leader on his team.

"There's not another receiver in the league I'd ever consider trading Michael Irvin for," Johnson said. "I think number one, he is a great player. I think he is a great competitor, a great practice player with great work habits, and I think that carries over to the rest of the players. The other thing is, personally, I like him."

So Irvin stayed, but was not the impact player after the injury. The Cowboys improved to a 7-9 record—even winning four games in a row and having a chance at the playoffs before losing their last two games. Irvin, however, was not much of a factor, finishing the season with just 20 catches for 413 yards and five touchdowns.

He hadn't lost his confidence, though. In his fifth game back, against the New York Jets, he lined up opposite cornerback James Hasty. Hasty said, according to a report in *Sports Illustrated*, "Michael Irvin! I have been waiting for this day all season."

"What have you been waiting for," replied Irvin, a whippin'?"

Irvin went out and caught four passes for 93 yards, including a 51-yard reception.

By the time the 1991 season rolled around, it was clear the Cowboys were ready to challenge in the NFC East. However, Irvin's three-year totals led many to believe that he just might not be able to live up to his promises of greatness.

"I don't doubt that's what people thought of me, but I've been hurt and I've been through three offensive coordinators and three different offenses in four years," Irvin said. "Now I've got an offensive coordinator, Norv Turner, who from Day One this year told me he believed in me, and I've got a great quarterback in Troy Aikman, who's really made a difference in my game. Troy knows all he has to do is put the ball in my vicinity and I'll go get it."

And that's just what Turner was counting on. "Other guys have better numbers and skill and people in the league like to evaluate a player on numbers," Turner said. "But Michael Irvin believes he is a great football player, and that's what he makes himself. He goes out and proves it every week."

The 1991 season saw the Cowboys return to the playoffs for the first time since 1985, finishing second in the NFC East with an 11-5 record. And Irvin became an All-Pro by enjoying one of the best receiving years in NFL history.

He led the league in receiving with a club-record 1,523 yards—the sixth highest receiving total in NFL history. Irvin was second in the league with 93 catches and also set a team record for consecutive 100-yard games (7).

In the playoffs, the Cowboys beat the Chicago Bears before losing to Detroit in the second round. Irvin was the Cowboys' leading receiver in the playoffs with nine catches for 167 yards. He also capped his season by being honored as the MVP of the Pro Bowl with eight catches for 125 yards and one touchdown.

Irvin's best streak of the season came in Dallas's final five regular-season games. During that span, he caught 37 passes, including 11 on third or fourth down, for 649 yards and four TDs. Against the Redskins, Irvin caught nine passes for 130 yards and one touchdown against Green. For days later, against Pittsburgh's Rod Woodson, Irvin caught eight passes for 157 yards and a score— a 66-yard dash that saw him change his route to avoid double coverage and break Woodson's tackle at the 10 yardline.

Daryl Green, one of the best cornerbacks to play the game, knows a good receiver when he defends one. "He's one of the best," Green said. "He's not the guy who knocks your socks off like

Jerry Rice, but he makes big plays. He's had success against me and that's a big deal."

When the season was all over, Irvin was as enthusiastic as he'd ever been about the future. "It's been such a long time coming," he said. "I love this game so much now. I wish the games were six quarters long, not four."

The best was yet to come—there were Super Bowls to be won.

5
SUPERBOYS

It all began coming together for Irvin—and the Cowboys—in 1992.

Irvin was quickly becoming a celebrity in Dallas. He had endorsements, TV deals, radio show appearances, and a city of football fans all idolizing him. This was everything Irvin dreamed would happen when he first came into the NFL. He still wore the jewelry and flashy clothes to go with his broad smile, and almost always took some time to sign autographs.

Rather than test the free-agent market, Irvin agreed to a three-year, $3.75 million contract before the season began. He put that behind him and concentrated on the next goal—getting to the Super Bowl.

Coach Jimmy Johnson had Dallas running on all cylinders. Norv Turner was still in place as offensive coordinator, Dave Wannstedt was defen-

Irvin's best day as a pro may have come on September 21, 1992. Although Phoenix's Lorenzo Lynch prevents a big gain on this play, Irvin caught eight passes for 210 yards and three touchdowns.

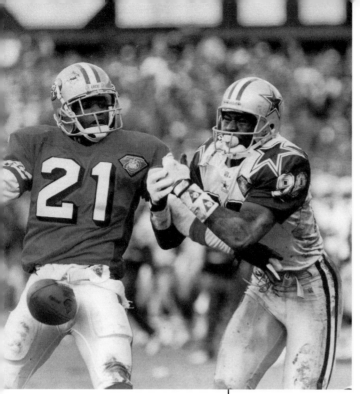

When Deion Sanders and Irvin first met, they were opponents, not teammates. In the 1995 NFC championship game, Sanders kept Irvin from catching this would-be touchdown pass.

sive coordinator and Aikman-Smith-Irvin were ready to become the most awesome trio in the game. There also were budding stars such as wide receiver Alvin Harper, tight end Jay Novacek, and guard Nate Newton. The defense boasted linebacker Ken Norton, Jr. and end Tony Tolbert.

The Cowboys made easy work of the regular season, compiling a 13-3 record in winning the NFC East. Their only losses were to the Eagles, Rams, and Redskins as they outscored the opposition 403-243.

Irvin had another stellar season, with 78 catches for 1,396 yards and seven touchdowns. He was second in the league in yardage, with his best outing against the Arizona Cardinals, when he had eight catches for a career-best 210 yards and three touchdowns in a 31-20 win. In that game, the Playmaker had scoring catches of 41, 4, and a career-best 87 yards.

But it was the first two games of the 1992 season that made the Cowboys believe in themselves. They opened with a win against Washington, but nearly blew a 34-0 third-quarter lead against the New York Giants before holding on for a 34-28 victory. In that game, Irvin had only four catches for 73 yards and one touchdown, but his biggest catch came late in the game. With the Cowboys clinging to a six-point lead with 1:40 left, Turner called a pass on third-and-7 at the Dallas 36. Aikman hit Irvin for 12 yards on a quick slant. First down. Game over.

Against the Cardinals the next week, receivers coach Hubbard Alexander recalled how keyed up Irvin was. "Michael said before the game, 'Ax, I feel it. I need the ball. These guys can't hold me,' " Alexander said. "It was like Michael Jordan in the first NBA final game. Mike was in the zone. The ball was looking bigger than a watermelon. I've never seen him come out of his breaks as quick as he did today [against the Cardinals]. People don't realize how he can just explode in and out of his breaks and separate from the defender."

In the playoffs, Dallas dominated the Philadelphia Eagles 34-10. More than 69,000 fans showed up at Texas Stadium for a pep rally the next Thursday.

Irvin was there, too. He told the crowd, "We have more people here than most teams have at football games. That's why most teams are home and we're going to San Francisco."

Dallas beat the 49ers, 30-20, and the Cowboys were on their way to the Super Bowl for the first time since 1981. In two playoff games, Irvin caught 12 passes for 174 yards, many of them for crucial first downs.

After the game, Irvin and Smith hugged. "They said it couldn't be done, Michael," Smith said. "We're in the Super Bowl, Michael, we're in the Super Bowl!"

Laughing, Irvin said: "I know, Emmitt. I know."

The Buffalo Bills knew Irvin was in the Super Bowl when he caught two touchdown passes late in the first half to put the game out of reach. Aikman was superb, while Irvin enjoyed what he called his most memorable game. Irvin finished with six catches for 114 yards. Aikman, the game's MVP, summed up what all his teammates were thinking when he said: "This is as great a feeling as I've ever had in my life."

The Cowboys were champions and all was right with the world. But even before the next season started, all was not right in Dallas. Dave Wannstedt left to replace Coach Mike Ditka at Chicago, and Emmitt Smith announced he would not show up in training camp until he had a new big contract, which Jerry Jones was not about to give him.

Dallas lost its first two games—to Washington and Buffalo—and many were ready to write off a Super Bowl repeat. After all, no team had ever come back from an 0-2 start to win the Super Bowl.

"I'm not great at losing," Irvin said at the time. "The day we lost to Buffalo, I remembered back to the way it was when I started here. I was like, 'here we go again.' "

The losses forced Jones to increase his offer to Smith. When Emmitt signed, Irvin was relieved. "With Emmitt here, I will be disappointed if we don't compete for the Super Bowl. We started 0-2 and everyone was crumbling around us. But we look around and see who we can beat."

They beat just about everybody, too, finishing 12-4 for the NFC East title. The Cowboys also gained the home-field advantage thanks to a regular-season, 26-17 win over the 49ers. In the victory, the Playmaker had a career-high 12 catches (for 168 yards and one touchdown), which helped offset a subpar game by Emmitt Smith. That came in handy at playoff time as the Cowboys beat Green Bay and then the 49ers to return to the Super Bowl for the second straight year.

"We wanted it and we went out and got it," Irvin said. "There were a lot of doubters out there. We never doubted we could do it."

Irvin was All-Pro for the third straight year. He was the league's second-leading receiver with 1,330 yards and his 88 catches were good for third place.

The Super Bowl found the Cowboys pitted against a familiar foe: Buffalo. With the Bills keying on stopping the pass, Dallas handed the ball to Emmitt Smith. The big man carried the ball 30 times for 132 yards and also caught four pass-

The dynamic duo of Alvin Harper (left) and Michael Irvin celebrate after their 1994 Super Bowl victory over the Buffalo Bills.

es. He was named MVP as the Cowboys became repeat champions with a 30-13 win.

After this Super Bowl win, there were more major changes in the works. Turner left to coach the Washington Redskins and a feud between Jones and Johnson intensified so rapidly that Johnson resigned and was replaced by former University of Oklahoma coach Barry Switzer, who had been out of football for five years.

Irvin was furious about losing his long-time coach. "I had been through the losing, and I wasn't going back, Irvin said. "I've been through 1-15 and 3-13 seasons, and I would not, will not, have any part of that. We were used to winning under Jimmy.

"I was upset, and it wasn't like I had a problem with Barry. I was upset with the situation. We had a car that was running perfectly. Why do you take it to the shop? That was my problem. I've seen what losing does to a football team and a town. Jimmy came in and changed it around. I didn't see any rhyme or reason for that happening."

But it happened and the players had to live with it. There was so much talent on the team, that many people thought it didn't really matter who coached the Cowboys in 1994. They were running so smoothly that it was tough to think about them not making the playoffs.

Even with a bunch of new coaches, the Cowboys surprised many of their critics and won the NFC East again with a 12-4 record. But this time, it was the 49ers led by Steve Young and Jerry Rice, who beat the Cowboys 21-14 to regain the all-important home-field advantage in the playoffs.

And there was Irvin, one of the first to defend Switzer. "Any other rookie coach comes in and takes a team to the championship game, he gets all kinds of praise," Irvin said. "But what they're saying here is, we should have been there anyway. The truth it, Barry did a great job of just keeping things together."

Irvin again surpassed 1,000 yards (79 receptions for 1,241 yards and six TDs) and the Cowboys reached their third straight NFC title game after beating Green Bay 35-9. In that game, Irvin had six catches for 111 yards as three Dallas receivers topped 100 yards in receptions.

The 49ers, though, were finally able to derail the Cowboys as they bolted to a 21-0 lead early in the first quarter and held off a furious finish by Dallas for a 38-28 win. The loss was a tough blow to the Cowboys' psyche, especially after such a glorious run of success.

Irvin was spectacular in defeat. He set club playoff records with 12 catches for 192 yards and two touchdowns. And as the game was ending, Irvin and Smith could be seen hugging once more. This time, it was for a different reason.

"I remember sitting down right before the end of the game and thinking, 'I cannot believe we are at this point,' " Irvin says. "We just started hugging each other, and I remember Emmitt saying, 'Mike, don't go. Don't leave me here. We're going to be all right.'"

If Irvin had any thoughts of leaving, they disappeared at that moment. "This is the same team I won two Super Bowls with," he said. "This is the same team I went to battle with time and time again. You always hear that there's no loyalty. That's not me."

So before the 1995 season got into full swing, Irvin signed a five-year, $15 million deal and vowed that he and the Cowboys would return to the Super Bowl. It didn't take long, either.

6
WINNING UNDER PRESSURE

This was the season that couldn't start soon enough for Irvin and the Cowboys. After their demoralizing loss to San Francisco in the NFC championship, Dallas was left with only one goal: Win the Super Bowl. Nothing else mattered.

As usual, it was a rocky road for the Cowboys —and Irvin. Even when Dallas was winning, there always seemed to be a bigger story or some sort of controversy. There was the signing of free-agent Deion Sanders away from the 49ers; Cowboys owner Jerry Jones defying NFL rules and signing his own marketing deal with Nike Inc.; two players being suspended for violations of the league's substance abuse policy; injuries; almost weekly criticism of coach Barry Switzer; and growing dissension between quarterback Troy Aikman and Switzer.

Michael Irvin had not been happy to see his old coach, Jimmy Johnson, leave the Cowboys. But he gave new coach Barry Switzer a hug after the Cowboys beat the Green Bay Packers in the 1996 NFC championship game.

The most controversial moment came late in a game against the Philadelphia Eagles. Both teams were fighting for home-field advantage in the playoffs, and late in the game the score was tied at 17-17. Dallas had the ball in Eagle territory and on fourth down, Barry Switzer had a tough call to make. He decided not to go for a field goal as he had lost faith in his kicker. Instead he sent out Emmitt Smith to try to rush for the first down. The Eagles held, though, and marched downfield to kick the winning field goal. Switzer's decision was savaged by second-guessers across the country.

Although Dallas finished with a 12-4 season and another NFC East title, the Cowboy's success seemed more of a sideshow than the main attraction. It was left for Irvin, who enjoyed his best season, to separate the issues the best way he could. Naturally, he did it in his own brash style.

"No, we don't have anything to prove," Irvin said before their playoff game against the Philadelphia Eagles. "We've got goals we set, and we'd like to go out and accomplish those goals. That's just it. I'm not going out saying, 'Hey, we did this to show the world.'

"I want to win for selfish reasons. I've got my own personal reasons. We wanted to win here, in Dallas. We wanted to play here, in Dallas. For selfish reasons, we wanted to play in front of our fans. And that's true. We don't have anything to prove to anybody."

In 1995, the Playmaker had another stellar season. Eighty-eight of his 111 catches were for first downs and 27 came on third or fourth downs. He was named to the Pro Bowl for the fifth year in a row and set an NFL record with 11 100-yard receiving games. When times are tough, Irvin didn't ask for the ball, he demanded it.

"Not only do my guys see me catching balls— it's easy to do that—but in crucial times, I will come in the huddle and they'll all look at me and say, 'Hey, Michael. We need this, Mike,'" he said. "I'd rather catch 10 of those balls during the season than to have 25 catches when they didn't look at me.

"You know why? If I make that play, then when it's third and 1, and I look at them and say, 'I need movement,' they feel obligated to get movement, and we get the first down. That's how you raise the level of everybody around you."

Irvin said he didn't need any extra motivation in the postseason. "I don't need to ready anything on the bulletin board," he said. "I don't need Jerry Jones, the owner, to come and say, 'Michael, here's $15 million to $20 million to play the game.' And I say, 'OK, I'll play the game.'

"I don't need that type of stuff. I play the game every day. I play the game in practice; I play the game. That's the difference. It's just a fine line between good and great; there's your fine line. Maybe the good players need it. The great players play the game."

Carnell Lake is late in applying the hit, but Irvin has already lost control of the ball. It didn't matter. The Cowboys beat the Pittsburgh Steelers in 1996 to win their fifth Super Bowl.

In 1996, Irvin was charged with possession of cocaine. He later pled guilty to lesser charges.

With the Eagles soaring following a 58-37 win over the Detroit Lions in the opening round of the playoffs, Irvin began to realize that one bad game would end another season short of reaching the goal.

"...Every playoff game that goes by, you get more and more scared because the closer you get to your goal...it's like, 'I'm right there.' There's nothing worse than to be right there and not get it.

"...But any athlete worth anything, any team worth anything, should enjoy those pressure moments. That's what the game is all about."

They easily beat the Eagles and next got to face the Green Bay Packers, fresh from a 27-17 upset of the 49ers. Again, the Cowboys prevailed 38-27 in the NFC championship game. But the Packers and quarterback Brett Favre gave Dallas all it could handle as they had a 27-24 lead before the Cowboys took control.

Once again, Irvin played a big part in the victory with seven catches for 100 yards, including first-quarter touchdown catches of 6 and 4 yards that put Dallas ahead 14-3. He was so elated that his team had reached the Super Bowl for the third time in four years, he went on national TV to defend his coach, the same coach he had criticized after he replaced Johnson in 1994. His intentions were good, but the words did not come out right.

"He takes all the bleep, all the maligning. Give him his due!" he declared. His comments, along with offensive remarks on national TV by Pittsburgh's Greg Lloyd, drew a reprimand from the league office. Even Irvin's mother Pearl was quoted as saying: "I will be talking with my boy. I don't need to tell you he didn't learn to speak that way in this house. I almost fell through the floor the first time he said it. I have never in my life heard Michael talk that way."

Another week, another controversy. That's the way it seemed in Cowboyland. And, as the Cowboys prepared for yet another Super Bowl, Irvin discussed how he felt about returning to the NFL title game after a year's absence.

"We're not going to the Super Bowl; we're going home," he said. "We let somebody borrow it as home last year. We've got to check the lease and see if they left it dirty. But it's home, period. Where we belong."

During Super Bowl week in Phoenix, Arizona, Irvin was unusually quiet. While Deion Sanders, Nate Newton, Troy Aikman, and others basked in the spotlight, Irvin kept a low profile early in the week. In fact, on the biggest interview day of the week, Irvin excused himself and left early, after about 10 minutes of answering questions about playing the AFC champion Pittsburgh Steelers.

He warmed up later in the week. He said it was great for the Cowboys to be back in the Super Bowl, but was counting on a victory to make it a successful return.

"Once you get there, there is no stopping," he said. "There is no happiness anywhere short of the Super Bowl. We said that last year. When I talked to Troy, he said, 'Mike, this season isn't complete unless we're in the Super Bowl.' Then Jerry Jones comes out, the shrewd businessman Jerry is, and said, 'if this team doesn't get to the Super Bowl...' Did he put pressure on us? No, he didn't because he knew that's what we expect from ourselves. So we were OK with that."

One of the final questions put to Irvin before the Cowboys played the Steelers was this:

Irvin wants to be remembered as a winner. Here he rides on a float during a parade that honored the 1996 Super Bowl champions.

"Michael, are you getting a little bored with all this?"

"No. Not at all. Bored of what? Playing? At this time of year? If I say I am bored, maybe God would show me next year, or the year after that or the year after that. 'Mike, you were bored, so let me take it away. Let me let you sit home while somebody else plays.' And I don't want that. I am not bored. I love what I'm doing. I love playing the game."

And Aikman sure is glad to have Irvin on his side.

"I think sometimes because of some of the personalities we have on this team our work ethic is understated," Aikman said. "Michael works as hard as anybody on our football team. He's extremely talented. He's a big, physical guy. He uses his body as well as anybody I've seen positioning himself from defenders."

On Super Bowl Sunday, Irvin went out and played the game. On the second play from scrimmage, he caught a 20-yard pass from Aikman on the Dallas 49 yardline. It set up a field goal and gave the Cowboys a quick 3-0 lead.

The next time the Cowboys got the ball, Irvin snared a key third-and-7 pass for 11 yards that led to a touchdown and a 10-0 lead. And on the Cowboys' next possession, early in the second quarter, Irvin caught a 12-yarder to keep the drive alive. Later in the drive, on a first down from the Steelers' 24 yardline, Irvin leaped in the endzone and made one of his patented catches for what appeared to be a touchdown. However, Irvin was called for offensive pass interference and the score was called back.

The Cowboys ended up with a field goal, led 13-7 at the half and held on for a 27-17 victory when Steeler quarterback Neil O'Donnell threw two interceptions right into the hands of Larry Brown. The celebration was on.

"This is the sweetest one of them all," Irvin exclaimed. "You can put the other two together and this one outweighs them. And that's because of what we went through all year."

The 1996 campaign was not nearly so wonderful for Irvin or the Cowboys. Before the season began, he was charged with possession of cocaine and pleaded guilty to lessor charges, which prompted the NFL to suspend him for the first four games of the regular season. His ultimate return to the gridiron helped spark Dallas to a playoff berth. But the Cowboys fell in the postseason, and there was no Super Bowl celebration for them in 1997.

Getting ready for his tenth season, Irvin has established himself as the Cowboys' greatest receiver. He already holds team records for career yards, receptions, consecutive games with at least one catch, and number of 100-yard receiving games. With three more years left on a five-year, $15 million contract, Irvin hopes his work ethic and desire will keep him at the top of his game for years to come.

However, he still dreams about someday returning home to play in Miami for his former college and pro coach Jimmy Johnson, who recently replaced Don Shula as coach of the Miami Dolphins. He realizes that's not going to happen, at least in the near future.

"I've got commitments here in Dallas," Irvin says. "I love Dallas and the people there. Don't get me wrong. I love South Florida. That's where my heart is. That's where my Mom is. But my job is in Dallas."

He may have another home waiting when his playing days are over—in the Pro Football Hall of Fame, in Canton, OH.

STATISTICS

MICHAEL IRVIN
Dallas Cowboys

Year	NO.	YDS	AVG	LONG	TD
1988	32	644	20.4	61	5
1989	26	378	14.5	65	2
1990	20	413	20.7	61	5
1991	93	1,523	16.4	66	8
1992	78	1,396	17.9	87	7
1993	88	1,330	15.1	61	7
1994	79	1,241	15.7	65	6
1995	111	1,603	14.4	50	10
TOTALS	**527**	**8,528**	**16.2**	**87**	**50**
PLAYOFFS					
1991	9	167	18.6	25	0
1992	18	288	16.0	33	2
1993	16	215	13.4	27	1
1994	18	303	16.8	53	2
1995	13	185	14.2	36	3
TOTALS	**74**	**1,158**	**15.6**	**53**	**8**

NO.   Number of receptions
YDS   Yards
AVG   Average
LONG   Longest reception
TD   Touchdown

MICHAEL IRVIN
A CHRONOLOGY

1966   Born on March 5, in Fort Lauderdale, FL

1984   Enrolls at the University of Miami

1985   Helps lead the Hurricanes to a 10-1 record and a Sugar Bowl appearance

1986   Miami enjoys an 11-0 season, but a loss in the Fiesta Bowl denies them a national championship

1987   Irvin again leads Miami to an undefeated season; the Hurricanes beat Oklahoma in the Orange Bowl to win the national championship; Irvin is drafted by the Dallas Cowboys

1991   Irvin sets a team record of 1,523 yards receiving and leads the NFL in yards per catch (17.9) and yardage; an All-Pro for the first time, Irvin is also named the MVP of the Pro Bowl; the Cowboys return to the playoffs for the first time in six years

1992   Sets a personal best of 8 passes for 210 yards and 3 touchdowns in a game against the Cardinals

1993   Helps lead Cowboys to a victory over the Buffalo Bills in the Super Bowl

1994   Cowboys win back-to-back Super Bowls, again defeating the Buffalo Bills.

1995   Signs a five-year, $15-million deal with the Cowboys before start of season; at end of season, is named to his fifth Pro Bowl

1996   Cowboys again win the Super Bowl, this time besting the Pittsburgh Steelers; Irvin is charged with possession of cocaine and pleads guilty to lesser charges; with Irvin suspended by the league for four games, the Cowboys start the season poorly; Irvin's return sparks the team and they return to the playoffs

SUGGESTIONS FOR FURTHER READING

Bayless, Skip. *The Boys*. New York: Pocket Books, 1993.

Fisher, Mike. *The Boys are Back: The Return of the Dallas Cowboys*. New York: Summit Books, 1993.

Shapiro, Leonard. *The Dallas Cowboys*. New York: St. Martin's Press, 1993.

ABOUT THE AUTHOR

Richard Rosenblatt is the National College Football Editor for The Associated Press in New York. He has covered college and pro football for 16 years. He covered University of Miami football from 1983-88 for The Miami News. He and his wife Jenny have two children, David and Erica, and reside in Floral Park, NY.

PICTURE CREDITS: AP/Wide World Photos: 2, 8, 11, 15, 19, 22, 26, 34, 36, 39, 44, 49, 52, 55, 56, 58; Archive Photos: 12, 46; Florida State University Archives: 16; Palm Beach Post: 29.

INDEX